Stealth Mode Persuasion

How to Persuade and Influence Anyone without Being Detected

By James T. Kent

Table of Contents

Introduction

In a perfect world, everything goes your way. But sadly, the real world is far from perfect. Often you want or need something in life, and there is often just one person in your way. Or perhaps you have a job in sales and need to learn how to persuade customers to buy products so that you can make a decent commission. These are reasons why persuasion is an art that you absolutely must hone to do well in the world.

Persuasion is never easy. You need something, and someone does not want to give it to you. You have to find the best way to convince the person to give you what you need. But sometimes, the very act of persuasion can result

4

in a solid no. This is where stealth mode persuasion comes into play.

The word "stealth" carries with it many negative connotations. It implies sneakiness, deceit, and even manipulation. But stealth can also serve you very well. Learning how to be stealthy is not always a bad thing. Stealth can enable you to achieve many things, including convincing others to do what you need.

People hate being persuaded. Once they say no, they want you to respect their answer. Stealth persuasion is a good way to get people to change their minds without feeling that they are being actively persuaded. You can change someone's mind in your favor without crossing boundaries or stimulating their resistance.

Persuasion also has some negative connotations. Typically persuasion is thought to involve pleading and begging someone to do something or to see something your way. But this method of persuasion is rarely effective. It is far better to be stealthy. Influence people to come up with the idea you want them to. Get them to see things your way by showing them how logical you are.

But, most of all, never be obvious that you are persuading people. Some of the most effective stealth persuasion may not even seem like persuasion. Being discreet is the secret to stealth persuasion.

These methods work far better than simply begging someone on your hands and knees. They also hurt your pride less. But how can you stealthily persuade someone? Many people have no clue how to start, and that is why they are poor at persuasion.

Use this book as a guide for some of the best methods to persuade others to do your bidding. With the tips contained in these pages, you can easily attain a stealthy and clever way to persuade others. If you have no clue how to start, do not wait any longer. Stealth persuasion can make a tremendous difference in your life once you learn how to do it right.

This book is a valuable start. Once you finish it, you can begin to practice on others. Then you will become a master at stealth persuasion. People will no longer be able to throw hitches in your plans. And you will feel better about yourself and your life.

Chapter One: Why Persuade When You Could Just...Influence?

Becoming a master of persuasion is the best way to proactively go after what you want. But when you begin practicing stealth persuasion, you will quickly learn that influencing people is the best way to go about it. True masters of manipulation can smoothly sway people to do anything, but if you are a beginner, it is best to start with the simpler methods of influence. To become successful at influencing people, you should work on building a few excellent influencing methods first.

When developing the art of influencing people, it is essential to develop a comprehensive understanding of human psychology. Using human psychology is the best way to get inside peoples' minds and encourage them to do what you want. A good way to learn how to influence people using their own psychology is to study Robert Cialdini's Six Influences. These influences are your toolkit to successfully influencing people. You can use these influences to convince people to do what you want without getting in over your head.

Reciprocity

The first method, reciprocity, may seem somewhat cold at first. Sadly, it is built off of the cynical viewpoint that nobody does anything out of true altruism. If someone does something, it is exclusively for their own personal benefit.

This may not seem like a very nice viewpoint. It allows for practically no faith in humanity. But when you are learning the art of stealth persuasion, faith in humanity has no place. You are in need of stealth persuasion because people do not act on altruism. If people did, then they would do things for you without any questions, merely acting to help you. Unfortunately, life rarely works this way. Instead, it is best to give up on altruism and understand that people usually operate on a system of give and take. They only give if they receive what benefits them in the end.

Reciprocity is basically a barter system, a system of obligation. By doing something for someone, you make them feel obligated to do something for you in return. Reciprocity is why businesses have free giveaways and offer complimentary drinks or candy. By giving customers something, businesses hope to influence customers to want to give something back by making a purchase or paying for a service.

Something as small as offering complimentary candy has surprising power over people. You do not have to do huge, extravagant things for people to give them a sense of obligation. There is no need to spend massive amounts of cash or spend hours of your day for people to get favors out of them. But you do need to take action and make a noticeable effort for others. Make people feel that you are doing something for them, so that they feel more inclined to do something for you. The term "You scratch my back, I scratch yours" is the informal essence of this exchange.

If you are attempting to get someone to do something for you, make sure to find out something that they may need first. Say you want a co-worker to cover you. First make sure that you are always pleasant to your co-worker and perhaps cover a shift for him first, or perform some other little favor at work. Maybe be the person that always orders pizza for the office or has the community candy dish on your desk. Of course, always be the person with a huge smile and something nice to say every day. When your co-worker sees that you do things for him, then he will most likely feel obligated to do something nice for you eventually.

With this influence tactic in mind, it is a great idea to rack up favors whenever and wherever possible. When you see an opportunity to do something for someone, do it. That way, many people are in a position to feel obligated to you. This is how you can have success with many different people when you find yourself needing to persuade them for favor.

Consistency and Commitment

Human beings crave consistency in life. There is nothing more frightening to a person than having cognitive dissonance, which is a state of mind where beliefs and actions do not mesh. Cognitive dissonance leads to doubt, confusion, and a general sense of unease or even panic. To avoid this panic, people are capable of shifting their internal self-beliefs to match their actions and their environment. People will force consistency into their lives because they need it so strongly.

"Fitting in" is one of the most common and classic examples of how people change their beliefs to fit their actions. Kids who feel out of place at school will start to change their actions to fit in with the "cool" group. But fitting in with the cool kids may require them to act in ways that jar unpleasantly with their morals. A nice kid may have to alter his morals about how stealing and bullying is wrong to avoid the constant guilt of a cognitive dissonance between his morals and how he behaves with his new group of friends.

Another good example is how people must adopt more racist attitudes when in prison, or in situations where racism is rampant. Fitting in with the new situation calls for a conscious shift in morals and beliefs to fit actions.

With these examples in mind, it becomes clear that changing someone's environment can change who they are. This is a scary fact, but it is also a chillingly powerful form of influence. If you use this influence just right, you can truly influence how people behave around you, and hence what they will do for you.

You can change people by how you treat them. You can treat them like an ally or best friend, and they will gradually become just that. The more you treat them with respect and dignity and praise their worth, the more they strive to be worthy. If you want someone to do things for you, consider treating them as if they are special. Make them feel that you value them and that only they can give you what you need. When people feel special, they do their best to act like they are, in order to cut out the cognitive dissonance telling them that they are not as special as you think. In time, you can groom people to want to be your special little helper.

Conversely, it is possible to manipulate people into feeling that they are not good enough. By making people feel that they are beneath you, they are more likely to listen to you as a superior. Then they will not fight you when you need something. However, be careful with this. Making people feel stupid or lesser than you somehow is a good way to push people away. People hate feeling like they are not good enough, and they may run away from you in order to feel better about themselves.

Remember to always be consistent in how you treat others. This consistency can cement their self-beliefs toward you. Eventually you can use this to your advantage.

Social Proof

Social proof is another one of Cialdini's influences which uses the concept of "fitting in." It is also a rather cynical influence, but it is based upon truth. This truth is that human beings are naturally herd creatures. Humans like to relate to other humans, to have others around them, and to be accepted by their species.

In order to be part of the herd, people will observe and copy the actions of others in a desperate attempt to be accepted. People rely on those around them for social cues about what is acceptable behavior and what isn't. They will base their decisions off of those around them, rather than make decisions on their own. Therefore, people are willing to change themselves to conform to the crowd. They will even do things that they know are wrong just because everyone does.

This herd mentality, or social proof, has tremendous power over people. This is why social proof is a prime advertising ploy. Have you noticed how ads always depict groups of people, smiling and having a great time? Commercials always show people being social. Clothing companies make their garments enticing by showing groups of glamorous women dressed in their wares, walking along the street or the beach, flashing their pearly whites and waving their long hair. Allergy commercials show people barbecuing and hanging out in their yards. These commercials work by indicting how you can fit in and relate with your peers by using certain products.

As a result of social proof, having plenty of friends results in others responding better to you. People see how you have a successful social life, and thus they believe that you are someone worth knowing. They are more likely to like you and to do things for you if you are surrounded with others who like you. Essentially, people will watch others for clues on how to behave, and if they see others treating you like a great person, then they will, too.

You can follow advertising's lead and use social proof to your advantage when persuading others. You can easily use social proof to convince people that they should do something for you to fit in with the crowd. The more socially accepted you are, the more others want to like you. The more others like you, the more likely they are to respond to your influence.

Liking

The secret of politicians and successful entrepreneurs lies in their ability to network. Networking lets you meet people who can help you on your journey. But it has another powerful benefit: it allows you to get to know powerful, influential people.

It is often said that it is not about what you know, but rather who you know. This is certainly true. Being liked and known by certain people gives you privileges and influence. Powerful friends lend you the power that you do not have yourself. The more people that like you, the more influence you have. Your friends can listen to you and help you get what you want. Powerful friends will also make other people want to help you get what you want. Building a network of people that will carry you to where you want to go is essential to success in society.

But it is not always easy to get powerful people to like you. Getting people to like you is a difficult gamble. Not everyone will always take well to you. There are a few ways to increase your chances of making important friends, however.

The first lies in making an attractive first impression. Keeping up your appearance, dressing nicely, and staying fit all project the image that you take care of yourself and have a healthy sense of pride. This encourages people to want to get to know you. People are also less likely to be repulsed by you.

Another tip is to establish something in common with the people that you want to befriend. People tend to befriend those that they can relate to. Try your best to pinpoint things that you have similar. It could be something very common, such as baseball or football, or it could be more obscure, such as a taste for abstract art or rare cheese.

Finally, it is essential to be a generally trustworthy person. This helps you establish a trusting relationship with the person you are attempting to befriend. Just as you want to make people feel obligated to do things for you using reciprocity, the reverse can apply to friendship. Act on your feelings of obligation to create a relationship of goodwill and trust. In time, this can make the other person feel obligated to you as well. Your relationship can become a symbiotic one, where you both act to benefit one another and exchange favors like a special and very valuable currency.

Getting people to like you enables you to have a network that you can use to your advantage. It also shows the world that you are likable, which makes others like you. The wider your network grows, the more successful you will be because you have more people to rely on.

Networks are especially important in your career but they can be of massive benefit in your personal life and hobbies as well.

Authority

People need authority to give their lives direction and shape. It is human instinct to look to a leader for guidance, be that leader God or a president or a project manager. Therefore, people respond to authority with a great deal of respect. When people sense authority, they are likely to heed that authority's voice.

Some people are natural authorities. They stride into a room, exuding the essence of "alpha." Others are meek and exude more of a "follower" vibe. Meekness and sweetness may be preached in doctrine as ideal traits for people to possess, but in the real world, these traits do not lend you any influence over others. Rather, it is best to be confident and assert your authority.

Even if you are not a natural leader, learn to be confident, sure of yourself, and ready to take charge. Do not be afraid to tell people what to do. Do not be afraid to lend your knowledgeable opinions. This may not come naturally to you, but if you force it, eventually it will become a habit. The more authoritative and assertive you act, the more respect you will earn. You will notice that suddenly people are willing to do your bidding and treat you with more dignity than before. People will even go out of their way to make you happy by doing you favors.

The best way to persuade people is to influence them. This sounds obvious. But in practice, it can be challenging for some people. If you are an introverted type, being an authority figure can be extremely daunting. It is important to learn how to exert influence on others without apology. Demand what you want, and do not doubt yourself or feel guilty.

Scarcity

Another aspect of human psychology that is essential for influencing people is scarcity. People are naturally hard-wired to be competitive. Dating back to caveman days when people had to fight for food, people have a natural internal drive to fight for resources. The more scarce resources become, the more competitive people begin to act. Black Friday is a classic example of how irrationally violent people can become as they feel urgency to snag an awesome deal.

Even if resources are not truly scarce, creating a sense of scarcity can drive people to act. Therefore, scarcity can be used as a very effective method of influence and manipulation. It is a common business tactic to convince customers that supplies are running out or an offer will expire in twenty-four hours. This creates a sense of scarcity. Buyers feel that they must act sooner than later or they will miss out.

Scarcity can be also used as a means to ignite people into violence. Riots can be stirred up by ringleaders telling people, "Aren't you tired of watching the rich have everything, while you have nothing? Aren't you tired of eating the rich man's scraps?" War can be instigated by governments convincing their people that they should invade another country to gain valuable resources, such as oil and gas.

Politicians are experts at using scarcity to incite people into a sense of panic. Then, they offer a solution to the issue by promising to end the scarcity.

You can employ scarcity as means to get people to do what you want. Creating a sense of scarcity can have an amazing impact on how desperate people become. People will literally do almost anything to get to a resource before it runs out. Whether you wish to sell something or lead people into some sort of action, using scarcity can drive people to quickly do what you want.

Chapter Two: Body Language and Subconscious Tactics

Stealth persuasion is supposed to be so stealthy that people are not aware they are being persuaded and manipulated. Therefore, it is not surprising that stealth persuasion involves a high amount of subconscious manipulation. Many little things influence the human subconscious, from body language to certain ways of phrasing what you say.

It is believed that people communicate seven percent with words, and ninety-three percent with nonverbal communication. Nonverbal communication is the most crucial aspect of communication between people. It includes many different things, such as tone, facial expression, hand and body movement, and posturing. There is so much information in what people do with their bodies and facial explanations - far more than in what they explicitly say.

In turn, you are saying so much with your own body language and facial expressions. Nonverbal cues are such a huge part of human communication that you must consider your body language when you are communicating, especially when you are trying to stealthily persuade someone. Since you can't give it away that you are persuading someone, you must make sure that your body language works seamlessly with what you are saying. Conflicting words and postures can confuse people or even signal to them that you have a rabbit up your sleeve.

Powerful Postures

In the previous chapter, we discussed using authority as a way to influence others. This continues into our discussion of body language. Part of asserting your authority and getting others to respect you involves having a powerful posture.

It is important to always be confident. But confidence can look like a fake macho front when your body language looks insecure. Shrinking back from people, slouching as you walk, turning your shoulder to the person you are talking to, avoiding eye contact, and crossing your arms can all make you look like you are not truly confident.

To exude power and confidence, it is best to adjust your shoulders back, straighten your spine, thrust your chest out, and stand as tall as you can. Also, don't forget to hold your head high and hold eye contact without shame and without wavering. This is a power posture. It gives you the appearance of dominance over others.

Touching

Strategic touching is a surprisingly powerful way to connect with others and create a bond. People respond well to tactile touch. Touching can make them feel that they are cared about. It can also create the illusion of closeness. The closer people feel to you, the more likely they are interested in helping you. Touch can build your network and get people to like you, both of which are important aspects in influence.

Touch does not have to be excessive or intimate. A handshake, a hand between the shoulder blades when someone is leaning over next to you, a tap on the shoulder or arm during conversation, or a side hug are all small and simple touches you can use to create bonds with people.

Space

Proxemics is the study of how human beings use the space around them. Many people use the term "bubble" to describe their personal space. There really is an invisible bubble that people mentally erect around themselves. People set rules for how much their space can be invaded, and they are often very protective of their personal space. When this space is invaded, people can become very uncomfortable.

Public space is usually twelve to twenty-five feet away from a person. This distance is the appropriate distance to keep away from utter strangers. An apology is in order if you accidentally are forced to enter this public space, such as on a crowded subway or bus. People can become extremely uncomfortable when their public space is violated by people that they do not know well, and they will likely either move away or grow suspicious and defensive.

Social distance is a little bit closer, four to twelve feet. This is the space that people use when interacting with acquaintances, such as work colleagues. It is also an acceptable distance to use when trying to build a bond with someone for the purposes of stealth persuasion.

Personal distance is the distance that people keep from good friends and family. Usually one must be invited into this space. You cannot just enter it without invitation if you are not close to someone.

Intimate distance is exclusively used for intimate exchanges, such as sex, kissing, hugging, or whispering secrets. Encroaching on intimate space can be very upsetting for people when they have not invited you into it.

Entering personal space in an acceptable manner is a good way to create a sense of bonding with others. You can use space to your advantage in stealth persuasion. If you enter someone's personal space at the right time, you can create a sense of closeness and a more personal bond. This can make people feel more comfortable with you. However, you must take care not to invade people's space too much, or they will become uncomfortable. Read body language for signs that you may or may not enter someone's space. If someone is closed off from you, such as by keeping their arms crossed, then that is a good indicator that you should not come any closer. But if they are open to you and continually make eye contact, you may have the green light to get a little bit closer.

Nodding

People appreciate being listened to. When they get the sense that they are being listened to, they feel that they are valued. Body language can convey if you are really listening or not and if you are interested or not.

It is best to always listen to people. Rely on listening as a means to learn valuable information about the person that you can later use as a way to get what you want from them. But also use it as a way to gain their interest and affection. Make sure your body indicates that you are listening, however, or the speaker will not know if you really care or not.

Despite the subtitle, nodding is not the only way to convey responsiveness and listening. It is important to develop a listening posture. The best way to achieve this posture is to turn your body toward the speaker, maintain eye contact, and lean in toward them. Avoid crossing your arms and legs, as these poses can make a person feel that you are closed off from them. You could prop your head on your hand to indicate deep thought and focus.

Throughout the conversation, give a slight nod or say, "Uh-huh" or "Yes" every so often when the speaker slows down. Smile or express empathy in response to what they say. Be responsive, and the speaker will respond well to you in turn.

Mirroring

When human beings relate and like each other, they often mirror one another's body movements and gestures. This mirroring creates a sense of similarity. People like seeing similarity in each other. It also confirms to one another that they are accepted and that they like each other. Since humans are herd animals constantly looking for validation from others, similarity can satisfy their worry that they are not fitting in.

It is often a joke that married couples look exactly alike after many years of marriage, but actually this phenomena is caused by years of mirroring. Mirroring each other's facial expressions eventually led to their skin drooping and lines forming in the same places over the years. This indicates how people who like each other and share a strong bond will engage in mirroring.

Also known as the "chameleon effect," mirroring is easy to do. Just wait about two to four seconds after someone leans forward, leans back, or otherwise shifts. Then mimic the movement. This mirroring can help you forge the trusting bond that enables easier persuasion.

It is possible to overdo mirroring. You do not want to seem obvious about what you are doing. Mirroring too much can seem desperate, creepy, or even fake and suspicious. But subtly mimicking movements after a brief waiting period of a few seconds can make the other person feel like you like them and are accepting them. The fact you are following their lead can provide them with a false sense of dominance, which can be conducive to them giving you what you want.

Eye Contact

Eye contact is one of the most important parts of body language and covert persuasion.

There is a reason people call the eyes "windows to the soul." Indeed, eyes are incredibly expressive. And people rely on eyes to tell a great deal of information about others. For instance, people look to the eyes to tell if a smile is fake or genuine. Similarly, people rely on eye contact to determine if someone is telling the truth.

Unfortunately, people do not always read eye contact correctly. It is possible that you are lying, but if you hold eye contact, people are more likely to believe you. It is also possible that you are telling the truth, but you will not hold eye contact out of nervousness. As a result, no one believes you and people think you have something to hide. A lack of eye contact can also make people think that you are untrustworthy and not confident.

Therefore, eye contact is a crucial part of communication. You cannot present yourself as confident if you do not hold proper eye contact. It is essential to maintain eye contact with the people you are attempting to persuade. This gives them a sense that you are trustworthy, confident, and open. Also, eye contact can reveal that you are paying attention to the person you are talking to.

It is also not a bad idea to let a little bit of vulnerability out through your eyes. Revealing some emotion helps other people bond with you and connect with you. They see you as another human being, someone who feels, someone capable of empathy. That is how you can help build a more trusting bond with people.

Once you make eye contact with someone, it can become almost a power struggle. It essentially is a grown-up version of childhood staring contests: The first person to look away is the lesser person. Always maintain eye contact and be the last person to look away. This portrays confidence as well as power. People are more likely to trust and want to be near someone who is brave enough to maintain direct eye contact and clearly has nothing to hide.

The only time when direct eye contact can pose a problem is between two alpha males or even alpha females. Two powerful people who sustain direct eye contact may see it as a challenge for power. Only one person can win. Avoid putting yourself in situations such as this, where you stand to enrage or else lose to someone who values their power.

Framing

Framing involves phrasing your words in such a way that people are logically driven to give the response you desire. Rather than focusing on changing the main point, it is possible to change the frame, or the context, of what you are saying. That allows for persuasion.

Framing can be a bit complicated. Consider the following examples to get a firm grasp of what framing entails.

To convince a friend to come to a new restaurant with you, begin by describing the new restaurant. Offer details about how wonderful the new restaurant is supposed to be and what businesses it is near. Do this to put your friend's mind onto a new restaurant and delicious food. Then, propose you try the restaurant.

If you are trying to get someone to sign a petition for social change for you, start by talking about how messed up society is. Discuss how social change is necessary. Bring up recent and relevant news that can be alarming and disturbing. This way, you place your target into a frame of mind where he or she wants to effect change on society. They are then more likely to receive your petition well.

There are three elements to framing: placement, approach, and word choice. Placement is connecting with people at the right time. Approach people when they are tired, or scared by a recent event such as a terrorism attack. At these vulnerable times, people are more open to saying yes to change and to doing things.

Approach involves appealing to people by offering either a positive gain or loss that they will get from doing what you want. For instance, a weight loss ad's approach is convincing people to buy a weight loss product because of the loss it promises. A gym can approach people by offering weight loss as well as the gain of confidence, attractiveness, and muscle tone.

Word choice is also a sneaky and important aspect in framing. The way words are strung together can have a positive or negative effect on the listener. Always use word combinations that evoke positive images in the person you are attempting to persuade.

Contrast Framing

Contrast framing is a businessman's best-kept secret. This is the way in which business people can shift your focus of what you can afford onto the benefits you can get from a more expensive item. A good salesperson will never let you talk about or focus on price; rather, he will insist on the benefits of a more expensive item, such as a restoration of family values or an increase in home satisfaction.

When using contrast framing, you want to always shift the person's focus off of the negative. Plant it on what they could gain. Find what is dear to them, and then promise that they will get it if they do what you want.

Physical Framing

Just as framing lets you frame your words in a certain context, physical framing allows you to create a physical setting for your words. A physical setting can help put the person you are persuading into a certain frame of mind. It can put them in the mood necessary for them to say yes.

A classic example is proposing to your girlfriend in a romantic setting. Lighting candles or going to a swanky restaurant or standing somewhere beautiful are all settings that allow for romance. With this physical frame set, you are able to put your girlfriend in a romantic frame of mind. Thus, she is more likely to respond positively to your proposal and say yes.

The same works for seduction. Creating a sexy atmosphere is the best way to get your prospective partner into the mood. Providing an environment can shift their frame of mind onto sex. Sexual innuendos and dirty talk also works by physically framing someone's mind onto sex.

Another example is exposing people to the smell of food to put them in the frame of mind of wanting. Baking cookies in a house that you are trying to sell creates a physical environment of hunger for prospective home buyers. When they smell warm chocolate chip, they are more likely to want to buy your house because the cookie scent hungers them and puts them in a frame of mind where they want something.

Reframing

Reframing is the very opposite of framing. It is changing the frame that the other person is using against you. In essence, it is actively changing someone's mind. When someone expresses a thought that goes against what you want, then "reframe" his mind to fit what you do want.

If you ask someone to do something for you and they reply that it is a hassle, reframe their negativity by describing how the hassle could actually benefit them. For instance, having an employee work late could earn grumbles. But just reframe their griping by describing how they can earn overtime and look good in the eyes of the big boss.

When someone expresses an emotion about something, be sure to reframe it to your advantage. If someone is sad, reframe their situation to make them happy. If they are mad, reframe the situation to calm them down. Do whatever you can to get someone into the proper mood to be responsive to what you are trying to accomplish.

Ask Yes Questions

The more people start saying yes, the more likely they are to keep saying yes. As a result, it is essential to get people to start saying yes a lot. The best to do this is to set their minds on yes by asking them questions with a guaranteed yes answer.

For example, have you noticed how salespeople will ask you, "It's a nice day, isn't it?" Or "You like to save money, right?" These are questions that people are almost always going to say yes to. Once a salesperson gets customers to start saying yes, he puts their mind into a "yes" frame. That way they are more likely to respond yes to his sales pitch.

You can do this, too. Ask people more yes questions than no or open questions. In a way, this is framing. But it is also conditioning people to say yes and to think along more positive lines.

Congruence

Congruence is a unique method of getting people to agree to something. Congruence involves taking action before a decision has even been made. Taking this action can force the other person to agree to something because it already seems like the deal is closed.

When businessmen are attempting to get a contract or seal a deal, they often like to shake hands before the deal is closed. This drives the purchaser to subconsciously feel that the deal is already closed, and so they agree to make the purchase or sign the contract.

You can apply congruence to your persuasion techniques with quite positive results. For instance, if you are trying to persuade a friend to go to a certain pizza place but the friend is thinking Chinese, start walking in the direction of the pizzeria as you continue to discuss what to do. This movement toward the place you want to go is congruence and it can drive your friend to say yes to pizza.

Congruence usually involves physical action. But it can also entail verbal action. Talking like a deal has already been made and you are already an employee at a company is a great way to get the job at interviews. Say things like, "I can't wait to hear from you" or "I can't wait to start on this," long before the person even says yes. That way, you are influencing them powerfully to say yes.

Congruence does call for some subtlety, however. You can easily become too pushy with congruence. Do not immediately start using congruence when trying to close a deal with someone. Rather, show them how the deal benefits them and edge them toward a yes. Begin using congruence closer to the end of your transaction.

Fluid Speech

When persuading someone, confidence is key. Therefore, it is also key to remove little items from your speech that make you appear less confident. In everyday speech, people are notorious for using little meaningless interjections, such as, "Um" or "I mean" or "Like." Sadly, these perfectly normal, everyday phrases strip away your appearance of confidence. They make you sound unprofessional and unsure of yourself. This does not make a good impression when you are trying to convince someone that you are right and your way is best.

Instead of stammering and interjecting useless little phrases, practice fluid speech. Fluid speech is speech that flows smoothly out of your mouth. You seem like you know just what to say, and you are sure of every word you utter. Fluid speech projects confidence as well as a solid comprehension of the subject you are speaking about. This can make people look up to you.

It is also not a bad idea to expand your vocabulary. People are impressed by big words, but of course only if you know how to actually use them. Never use words you don't actually know the meaning of. Spend some time with a thesaurus or dictionary and learn some new words that can help you appear smarter and more knowledgeable. Your big vocabulary will help you impress those you are trying to persuade and will enable you to seem more fluid and knowledgeable.

Get People to Come to Conclusions Themselves

One of the most powerful ways to get people to see your view is to present them with information and ask questions that make them reach the realization you desire on their own. We already discussed this a little bit in the earlier section about framing. Framing questions is a useful way of getting people to come around to your way of thinking without forcing them to see things your way. But now we will delve deeper into this powerful strategy.

Consider this example. You make a generalized statement, something such as, "If you don't study, you'll never get into college." A statement like this leaves an opening for the other person to respond with an exception, such as, "Dad never studied and he's an engineer." Another example is telling someone, "You need

to go to bed or your growth will be stunted!"
They can easily just counter your statement by
telling you how someone they know is a night
owl and the tallest person in class.

Forcing your beliefs on other people only
encourages them to become defensive and reject
what you are saying. It can also make them feel
that you do not know what is best, but are simply
being bossy and pushy. This is a surefire way to
lose someone's interest in doing what you ask.

Instead, try to convince people of the logic
of your statements by having them reach the
conclusion you are trying to make themselves.
Feed them information and ask them questions
that bring them to the desired conclusion.

Back to our previous examples, imagine the response if you tweak how you talk to the person. Instead of making a disputable blanket statement, tailor a question to the person's unique situation. "How do you think you will do on your test if you don't study? Do you think you'll be able to get into that college you wanted?" Or "Do you think it's healthy to get so little sleep?"

Another application for this trick is getting people to feel that ideas are their own. If they feel that they can take credit for an idea, then they are more open to it. Nobody wants to always be the draft mule, working on others' ideas. Rather, people like to have a sense of being in control and in charge. Give people this sense when it comes to great ideas you have.

Ask for Help

Asking for help is a great way to make others feel needed and useful. When you ask for small favors from people, people feel that they are a special part of your team. This appeals to the herd instinct that all people share. If they feel like a part of a team, then they form a subconscious commitment to continuing to do things for you.

Asking strangers for help for huge things right off the bat is foolish. But once you start building rapport with people, then you can easily ask for small favors. Even if it is just running to the store or giving you a lift after work, these small favors can convert people into feeling like they are part of a team on your side.

Women especially can experience high rates of luck with asking men for favors. Men like to feel needed. They feel needed when women turn to them for car help, help moving, or other small yet important things. If you are female, you may find that batting your eyelashes at a man is a great way to get him to do anything for you. It is rare that a man will turn down your plea for help.

Foot in the Door

Much like asking for help and asking yes questions, "foot-in-the-door" is a manipulation or persuasion technique where you make a small request. When the person agrees, you then make your real request. The person has a harder time saying no since they have already said yes to your original request.

Try asking people for small favors, such as a ride or a trip to the store. When they say yes, then ask for something bigger. This technique takes some impudence and may result in failure sometimes. But people are surprisingly susceptible to guilt. They would rather please you than upset you. Socially, humans are very sensitive and hate saying no. Therefore, this method does have a high rate of success.

Offer a Warm Drink

To be effectively persuasive, it behooves you to appear warm and likable. Your behavior does a great job of conveying your warmth and likability. But sometimes even that is not enough. The world is a hard place and many people have developed deep skepticism as a form of self-protection. Not everyone is taken just by a warm smile or a firm handshake.

One easy trick to get people to subconsciously believe that you are warm and likable is to ply them with a warm drink. Especially in winter months, offer people coffee, tea, cocoa, a toddy, or some other hot drink. The warm cup between their palms makes them feel that you are also warm. Offering a warm drink can also indicate that you are hospitable and caring.

Similarly, offering a coat or jacket to someone in the cold is a great idea. This small act of kindness can help people come to trust you and want to help you.

Chapter Three: Get Inside of Their Heads with Psychology

Previously we covered the use of psychology and subconscious techniques in influencing people. Now we will talk about some other psychological tactics that can help you manipulate and essentially train people to do what you want. This is no longer influencing people, but rather actively changing their brains. In short, this chapter covers true manipulation.

Manipulation is normally considered immoral and wrong. Good people do not live entirely on manipulating others. Master manipulators are often considered sociopaths, cold and heartless people who view other people as objects to use rather than individuals worthy of respect and dignity.

But sometimes even the nicest person in the world must use manipulation. Life is not always easy and people are not always going to work with you. That makes manipulation necessary to get what you truly need from people who are staunchly refusing to do what you want.

Many people have their guards up against manipulation. The instant that they sense they are being manipulated, they can become enraged. It is essential to subtly and covertly go about manipulation in order for it to work.

Conceal Your Intent as Goodwill

To successfully manipulate a person, you must take care to disguise your manipulation.

One of the best ways to do this is to hide your true intentions, or your goals. Do not reveal what you want. In fact, do not reveal that you want anything at all. Rather, give the vibe that you are doing something for the other person.

There are many instances where this tactic of hiding the cards up your sleeve is used in daily life. One instance is when an employee goes the extra mile. The employee masks his or her extra effort as good hard work ethic and passion about the company, but really he or she is after a raise, promotion, or the boss's favoritism. Another good example is when a company treats you wonderfully, making you feel warm and fuzzy inside. Really, they just want your money.

People constantly are hiding their true intentions. If they didn't, they probably would never get what they truly want. The fact people use this manipulation tactic all the time proves that disguising your goals as goodwill is an effective and even a socially acceptable way to get others to do what you want.

Keep The Focus on the Other Person

No one likes to just sit there listening to you talk about yourself. This is especially true when you are trying to persuade someone. When you are persuading someone, you do not want to make them feel that the encounter is all about you. They will quickly lose interest.

Rather, it is best to keep your focus on the other person. The conversation should revolve around them. Ask them questions to get them talking. Find out what they like, and then ask them about it. There is nothing people love more than going on and on about subjects that interest them. If you make them feel that the conversation is all about them, then they will feel more warmly toward you. Then they are more likely to want to do things for you because you make them feel special and important.

When you are trying to manipulate someone, always act as if you are the most selfless and wonderful person on Earth. As people come to adore you, they always begin to do whatever you want. Your loyal following will result in multiple rewards for you. The only way to grow this following is by putting yourself aside for a while, at least on the surface.

Make Others Feel that They Have an Edge

Stealth persuasion is all about gaining an edge over others. You use this edge, be it reciprocity or guilt, to get people to do what you desire. Throughout stealth persuasion, you must always have this edge, no matter what. Without an edge, you have nothing to stand on and no way to manipulate the other person.

But one excellent manipulation tactic is to make the other person feel like he or she is the one with the edge. This is a great way to make people believe that they are dominating the situation and that you are innocent of trying to manipulate them.

One way to do this is to do lots of little things for someone. That way, the person feels that they have dominance over you, but they also feel guilty for treating you like a slave. As a result, you have a hidden edge over the person, but they do not realize it. They think they hold the edge over you.

Another way to do it is to get someone to do many small favors for you. The person thinks that you owe him or her. But the person is also in the habit of doing things for you and wants to continue as they wait for you to return their many favors. The longer they do favors for you waiting for a reward, the more of an edge they believe they have. But really you have the edge in this situation.

Conditioning

Conditioning is typically associated with Pavlov's famous experiments with dogs. The human brain is really no different than the canine brain in that it is hard-wired to respond to certain stimuli. It is possible to condition people to respond to stimuli just as Pavlov conditioned his dogs to salivate at the sound of a bell. This is known as classical conditioning and it is a cornerstone of human psychology.

In persuasion, you may be looking to get people to respond to you in a certain way. One way you can get people to do this is by conditioning them. When they do something you want, for instance, reward them with positive stimuli. This stimuli may involve touch, as people love physical contact. Or it could be a compliment or a gift, such as free candy or lunch.

Find out what people truly want, and then reward them with their desires for behaviors you want to encourage. For instance, if someone has a crush on you, reward them with a touch or some flirtation when they do what you want.

Relatively quickly, often after only one incidence, people will form an association between doing something for you and getting a reward. People will start wanting to do things for you. Make sure you provide the reward every time. This way, you are confirming the conditioning and keeping it fresh for the next time you need to use the person.

It is also possible to train people to respond to you with environmental stimuli. For instance, playing music someone likes whenever they do a chore for you can be an extremely effective means of getting them to always do that chore when you play their favorite music. People learn to associate behaviors and stimuli and will strive to behave in ways that result in their ideal rewards.

Gaslighting

Gaslighting is not the nicest form of manipulation. In fact, many people categorize it as a form of mental or emotional abuse. Do not use this tactic unless you are in a situation where you direly have to.

The term came from a 1938 Broadway play titled *Gaslight*. In the play, a man convinces his wife that she is insane by turning the gaslights in their house down but denying that he had changed the light settings at all whenever she asked. Through this subtle action, the man is able to manipulate his wife into believing that she is crazy and her perception of the world is false. It also enables him to have total control over her, by making her rely on him for a proper perception of the world.

Gaslighting can be very helpful if you want to get total control over someone. Someone is likely to do whatever you want if they feel that they must rely on you totally for an accurate picture of the world. The trick to gaslighting is to make someone doubt his or her own sanity and perception of the world. Like in the play, you can make someone feel crazy by proposing they make very real things up. You can also deny that what they see in the world is real. For instance, if someone insists that it is cloudy, you can laugh and tell them that no, it is sunny today. This is a very bold example, but more subtle methods can be employed to undermine someone's confidence.

Bribery

Bribery can be an effective means of manipulation if all else fails. Parents often bribe their children with the promise of a cookie after dinner if they wash dishes. Men may bribe women with a promise of love in exchange for sex. People will often do what you want if you offer them something they really want.

Bribery works best when you know a person well enough to gauge what their inner desires are. Some people are easy to read; others are more difficult. But almost everyone in the world just wants to be loved and supported. Use this knowledge to your advantage and offer affection, support, or kindness of some sort to people.

Garner Sympathy

One way to get an edge over people is to garner their sympathy. When people feel sorry for you, they operate on guilt and try to help you. The best way to garner sympathy is to make people feel like nothing is ever your fault but rather theirs.

If you are running late, claim that it is their fault for setting your meeting for a time that does not work well for you. Act as if it was an intense inconvenience for you to come at the time they chose. This can elicit their guilt and sympathy.

This is just an example of how you can make people feel guilty for anything and everything. When someone feels guilty, they also feel obligated. They are now in a position where you can successfully manipulate them.

Emotional Blackmail

Emotional blackmail plays on the wounds and scars that people carry inside themselves. Its main purpose is to make someone so distressed and miserable that they give in to you. Emotional blackmail, like gaslighting, can qualify as a form of abuse and is not advisable to use on your loved ones and people you care about. It causes a great deal of emotional pain. However, if there is someone that you hate or desperate times call for desperate measures, emotional blackmail can be extremely effective.

When you emotionally blackmail someone, you may use explosive anger as a means to frighten them into doing what you want. If that fails, you may switch to a happier mood and kindness that makes them tremble with relief. They will do whatever you want to keep you in the light mood and avoid more angry outbursts. The emotional back and forth exhibited by you can make the other person enter a "FOG," which stands for Fear, Obligation, and Guilt. While in this fog, people are more than willing to do what you want, just to avoid your sharp mood swings.

With violent mood swings, you can invoke fear in those around you. You can easily make them feel fearful and guilty of angering you. This combination gives you a form of emotional control over people that you can use to your advantage. Remember, this is not a way to make friends or to treat those you love. This is a heavy manipulation tactic that works best only on those you do not care about hurting.

Chapter Four: Why Persuasion Fails

Throughout this book, we have discussed how to successfully persuade others. Now we will go into some of the reasons why persuasion fails. This is the section that covers what NOT to do. Sometimes, learning what not to do is just as important, if not more important, than learning what to do. Therefore, this is an essential section that you must pay close attention to.

There are several reasons why persuasion may fail. A brief Internet search reveals many forums and advice posts, where people want to know why their best persuasion attempts always fail. Typically, the answers point to one of the following reasons.

Imposing Your Views on Others

The number one reason persuasion fails is because you were being pushy or forceful. When you try to impose your views or goals on others, you stand the risk of driving them away. You can create disagreements and reveal sharp conflicts of interest.

When using stealth persuasion, you must take care to never be pushy. Always be polite instead. You must also always keep the focus on the other person. This prevents you from appearing selfish and driving the person away.

Conflicts of interest are bound to arise between people with different worldviews. The best way to deal with conflicts of interest is to convince someone that there is a compromise. It is also a good idea to try to show them the benefit of your interests, while still respecting theirs. People are not likely to go out on a limb for you if you do not also take care of their own personal interests.

Revealing the Card Up Your Sleeve

Never, ever give it away that you are trying to persuade someone. Revealing the card up your sleeve is a good way to estrange people. People despise being manipulated or persuaded. If they catch you, they are not likely to take kindly to the incidence. Hiding the card up your sleeve is of paramount importance when using stealth persuasion on people.

Being Desperate

The last thing you ever want to do during stealth persuasion is to appear desperate. Desperation sets off internal alarms in other people. They see desperation, and they think something is wrong, either with you or with the situation you are in. They are more likely to run far, far away than to assist you in any way.

Confidence is far better than desperation. People respond well to confidence. When trying to persuade someone, never act desperate. Rather, act confident that what you need is the right thing. This is more likely to make someone feel comfortable about doing what you want.

Chapter Five: Saving Face When Persuasion Fails

After reading this book, you have all the tools to become a master at stealth persuasion. You can easily become practically a ninja at influencing others' minds, a practical Jedi of mind tricks. You will be able to influence people so that they are not even aware that you are trying to persuade them to do what you want. With stealth persuasion, you can be both smooth and convincing, and never make enemies.

But sometimes even your best attempts at persuasion may fail. They say "You win some, you lose some," and this saying is especially true when it comes to things like persuasion, where you are dealing with the fickleness of other human beings. Not everyone is going to respond to your techniques well. Not all of your techniques will go smoothly without a hitch.

Generally, people are more alike than they are different. Almost all human beings respond exactly the same to certain psychological tactics. Learning these tactics can greatly raise your chances of successfully persuading anyone. But sometimes, you may run into a person who is particularly savvy at evading manipulation. You may try to tackle a person with a unique mindset and psychological makeup, who simply does not respond normally to the techniques outlined in this book.

Occasionally, especially when just starting stealth persuasion, you may err in your technique and lose someone's favor. It is important to always be polite and gentle to avoid angering someone. People hate being manipulated so the last thing you want to ever do is let someone realize what you are trying to do. However, there may be cases where you fail in this endeavor.

Whatever the reason your persuasion tactics failed, this is not cause for despair. Do not beat yourself up or give up on stealth persuasion as another self-help fad that does not truly work. Stealth persuasion does work and you are just as capable of mastering the techniques as the most renowned diplomats and conmen. Treat your failures as chances to improve and fine-tune your skills. Use them to find out what does not work, and what may work on certain individuals.

Rationalize

Rationalizing is a way of passing off your actions as perfectly justifiable, even if they are not. Manipulation is not always a good thing. Perhaps when you manipulate someone, you feel a rift between your conscience and your actions, or a cognitive dissonance, which makes you uncomfortable. Probably your conscience is afraid of what other people will say. Certainly other people will say that what you are doing is wrong. If you are ever caught manipulating someone, you may have fingers pointed at you in anger, accusing you of being a bad person.

You are not a bad person. You are just doing what you need to do to get by. The world is a rough place and sometimes manipulation is the ideal way to get ahead. No matter why you are manipulating someone, understand that there is a valid reason for it. You do not have to tolerate being told you are doing something wrong.

This where the process of rationalizing, or justifying, your actions comes in handy. Instead of saying sorry or feeling bad, it is best to feel that you are not in the wrong at all. Then work at convincing others of that fact. Justify your actions by explaining that they were not as bad as everyone thinks, that you were not intending to manipulate anyone, and that you just really needed something.

Regain Favor

In the event that you are caught trying to persuade someone, you may lose favor. This is never a good feeling, nor does it bode well for your future manipulation attempts on that person. Therefore, it is crucial to repair damage when it occurs.

Always treat the person like they are special to you. Treat them with kindness and grace, throughout the manipulation process and afterward. Deny doing anything wrong and strongly feign innocence. While it is strongly unadvisable to apologize, you should if the person demands an apology. Rather than admitting to wrongdoing, simply say, "I am sorry for upsetting and hurting you." Then avoid trying to persuade this person for a while until their wounds and skepticisms heal.

Still Be Grateful and Polite

The best advice in any situation is to never burn bridges. When you burn bridges, you lose a person's favor forever. There is no way that you can regain their favor or win them back. You never know when you may need someone again. Therefore, always be sure to keep people in your favor, even when persuasion fails.

It is easy to lose your temper and burn bridges out of anger or frustration. Ideally, you should go into persuasion with no sense of entitlement. This frees you from the anger emotions that inevitably will rise if someone does not do what you feel entitled to. When someone fails to come through for you, you will be able to handle the rejection gracefully and not act out in anger.

Always continue to be nice and polite to the people you try to persuade, even if persuasion fails. Perhaps it failed this time, but next time you have established even more rapport with the person, and so you may achieve greater success later on. People will respond well to your grace and possibly even feel obligated to help you again. This leads us to our next section, about using guilt to your advantage.

While it is necessary to be graceful, it is not advisable to apologize. An apology is an obvious confession that you were in the wrong and that you were actively trying to manipulate someone. This admission only serves to give the other person an edge over you. In stealth persuasion, you want to always keep the edge, and never give it away.

Use Guilt to Your Advantage

Going back to reciprocity, it is possible to make someone feel obligated to help you. One way to do this is to make them feel bad for not helping you the first time. With this guilt, you have the necessary leverage to get someone to do what you want the next time.

Guilt is an incredibly powerful emotion. Guilt has the ability to haunt people for a long time. People will often feel guilty because they have betrayed their own kindness and their sense of obligation. Therefore, when the horrible emotion of guilt bubbles up, people will often be willing to act to make the feeling go away.

Earlier we discussed cognitive dissonance, which is when someone feels a conflict between their actions and emotions. If someone is kind but acts coldly, there is likely a cognitive dissonance occurring inside his or her mind. You can exploit this cognitive dissonance by making someone feel guilty and then suggesting a way that they can find solace for their guilt by doing something for you. Always spot cognitive dissonance as soon as possible, and use it as an edge.

First, always keep kindness in your heart for others. Go the extra mile to help co-workers, friends, and family. When people see how much you do for them, this creates the reciprocity we discussed earlier. If they do not reciprocate, people often feel guilty. You can casually mention something along the lines of, "Would you mind helping me with homework tonight? I know you said no last night, but I really need help and I helped you with your math last week."

This works by playing on their guilt for not helping you before, as well as asking them to reciprocate something nice you did for them previously.

Have a Plan B

People are fickle beings. It is never a safe bet to put all your effort and all your faith into one person. If that person lets you down, you have dedicated all of your time to persuading them and not to creating alternatives.

It is ideal to always create alternatives in life. This is especially true when you are trying to persuade someone. Do not focus on just one person. Have multiple people to persuade. Also have alternative methods of going about getting what you need, so that if someone says no, you are not left without options.

Learn When to Let Go

Usually, quitting is frowned upon. American society encourages drive and dedication until the end. Quitting is often viewed as the coward's way out, or the path of losers. The reason for this philosophy is certainly understandable. Dedication usually brings far more success than quitting. If you quit, there is no chance at all that you will succeed.

But sometimes, quitting is necessary. There is a time when you need to realize that pushing any farther will only hurt you. This can certainly be a useful sense to have when you are trying stealth persuasion.

Sadly, there are times when all of your attempts to persuade a particular person seem to be going sideways. There is just no way you seem to be getting ahead. Pushing on will only humiliate you and anger the person you are trying to persuade. When you begin to realize that there is no getting ahead and you are beginning to anger people with your persuasion efforts, it is time to consider quitting.

Force

If someone refuses to help you but you can't quit, it may be time to give up on stealth persuasion and instead employ force. Force can be physical. It can be emotional blackmail. It can even involve threats. IF there is something you need and you don't have time for games, force is the only option left. There is a reason heroes in movies usually resort to pointing guns at guards in order to break into top secret government facilities to rescue someone or end an evil scheme. They simply don't have time or patience for bargaining and persuading. Rather, it is time to draw out the guns and use some force.

Force is always a last resort. No matter how strong you are at physical or emotional force, there is always someone stronger. There is a high chance that force will not end well for you. Even if it does, forcefully getting your way is almost guaranteed to burn bridges. You will not likely have a friend anymore in the person that you used force on.

Conclusion

By now, you have hopefully gleaned some very useful persuasion tactics from these pages. You are on your way to being a master of persuasion and getting just what you want. Life can be much easier when you are able to persuade others.

You should also now be better equipped at dealing with failures in persuasion. Ideally you will never face a failure. But other people are, unfortunately, fickle creatures and it is sometimes inevitable that even your very best efforts will fail.

However, consider this book the very first lesson of a long and detailed trade. Like all trades, you can stand to learn more and more.

You are never entirely finished learning. The longer you work in the trade, the more you learn. You have the rest of your life to improve your persuasion skills. Many situations will arise, calling on your skills and granting you the opportunity to hone them. With each situation, you will acquire more confidence and more experience. In time, you will become excellent at persuasion.

It is important to always keep in mind that the tips in this book are offered as general guidelines, as opposed to strict rules. All people are different, but almost all people share similar psychological instincts. Instincts stem from caveman times and are embedded in human DNA. Therefore, using psychology on people is usually effective across the board. But sometimes, people respond to psychology differently. Some people are more aloof and able to detect and deflect manipulation; other people are more gullible and susceptible.

Therefore, it is necessary to tailor your approach to the individual. There is no one persuasion method that will work on every person, every time. If a particular attempt you make to persuade someone does not work well, do not despair and dismiss stealth persuasion as a means to get whatever you want in life. Stealth persuasion is still a very useful tool to possess, and it will serve you well.

Some of the material in this book has a cynical origin. A rather dark view of the human race is in order to arrive at some of the conclusions presented in these pages. The cynicism is not meant to depress you or make you hate your fellow man. However, it is necessary for a realistic understanding of human psychology, which is the cornerstone of successful stealth persuasion.

Many of us want to believe in the goodness and grace of humanity. We secretly cheer for good people and long for the existence of true altruism. This faith in the goodness of humankind is a noble thing. But it is also naïve.

While there are many examples showing how human beings can be altruistic and good people at heart, there are many more examples proving that people are usually only out for their best interests. Understanding this fact is cold, cynical, and not necessarily uplifting. But in combination with the tools offered in this book, this understanding can allow you to truly get inside the minds of other people. Guilt and naiveté will no longer be in your way.

It is important to always bear in mind that other people constantly try to persuade you as well. Every day, salespeople, friends asking for favors, and co-workers attempting to get you to do their work are just some of the people working on your brain to get you to say yes. With this in mind, you should not feel overly guilty about manipulating others. It is essential that you do what is best for you. Do not let anyone stand in your way; use persuasion to eliminate their obstinacy. And do not let guilt keep you from doing what is best for you.

Thank you for reading this book. Good luck as you learn how to use stealth persuasion to your advantage. After all, you deserve leading

the life you want without opposition.

www.ingramcontent.com/pod-product-compliance
Lightning Source LLC
Chambersburg PA
CBHW050410290526
45786CB00003B/1204